Lee Evans arranges George Gershwin

Second Edition

HAL•LEONARD® CORPORATION

7777 W. BLUEMOUND RD. P.O. BOX 13819 MILWAUKEE, WI 53213

EMBRACEABLE YOU

Words by IRA GERSHWIN
Music by GEORGE GERSHWIN
Arranged by LEE EVANS

Rubato (♩ = 72)

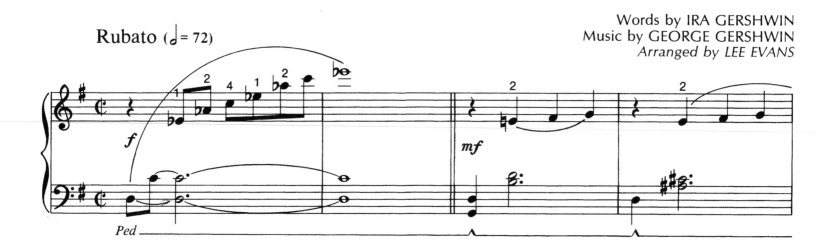

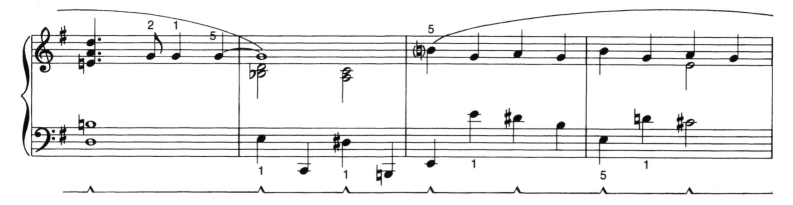

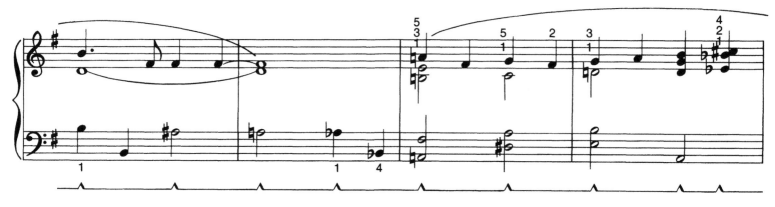

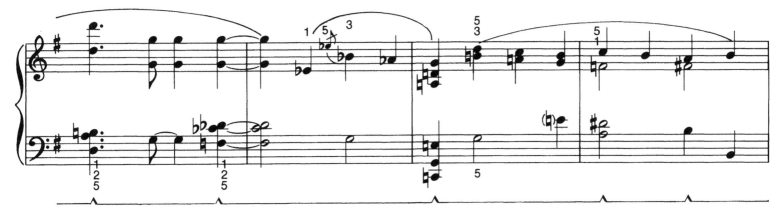

In tempo (rhythmically)

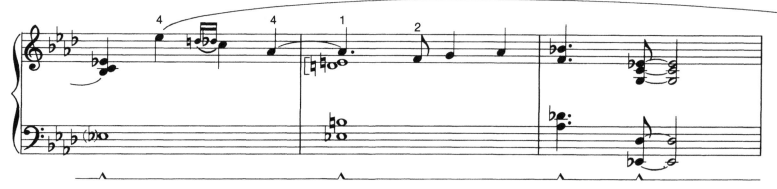

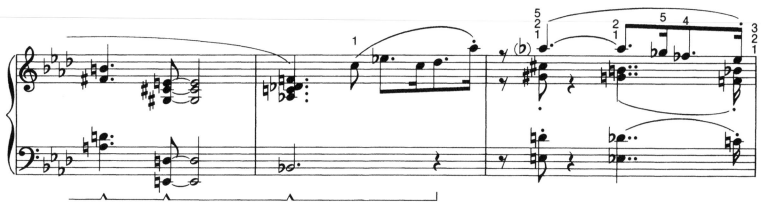

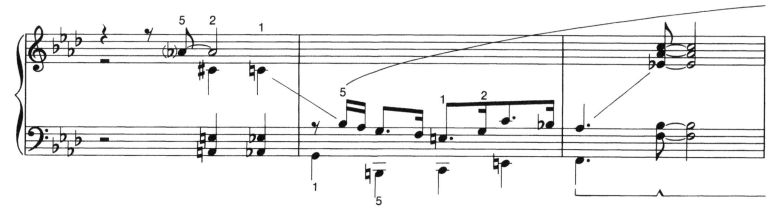

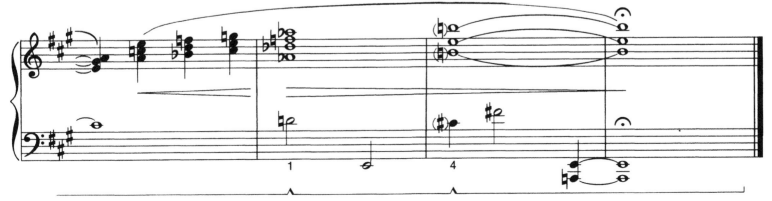

A FOGGY DAY

Words by IRA GERSHWIN
Music by GEORGE GERSHWIN
Arranged by LEE EVANS

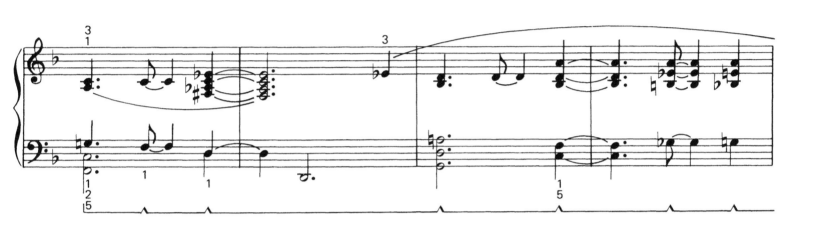

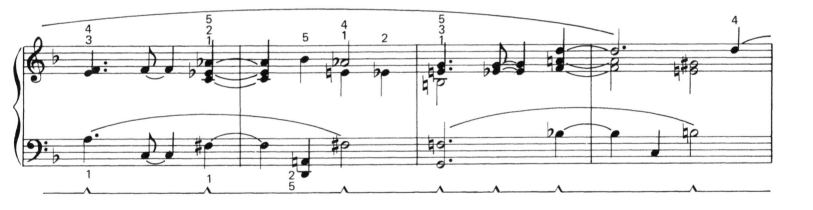

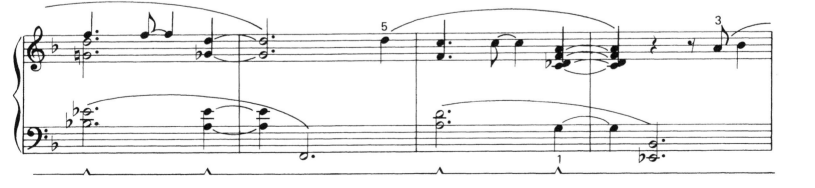

8

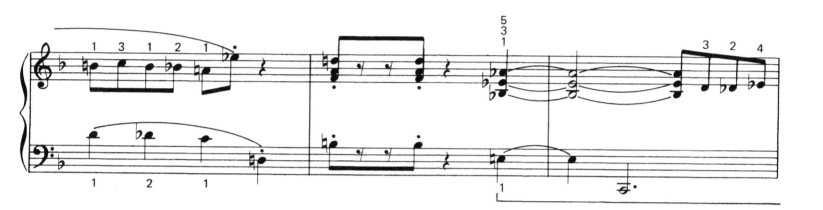

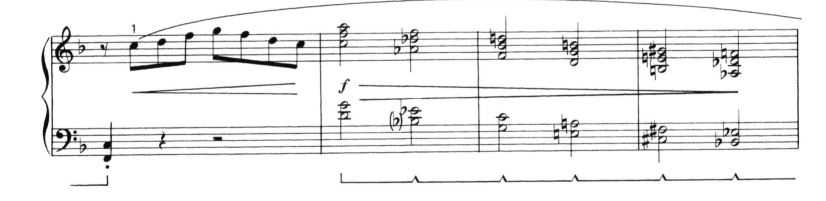

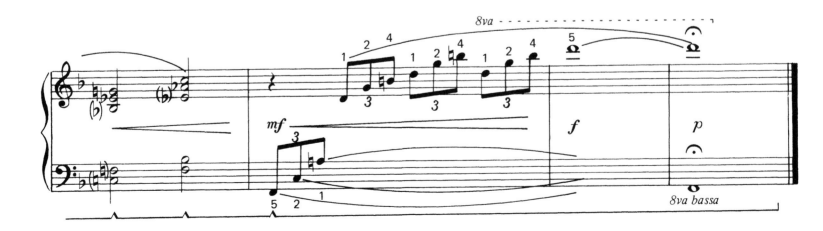

IT AIN'T NECESSARILY SO

Words by IRA GERSHWIN
Music by GEORGE GERSHWIN
Arranged by LEE EVANS

Moderato scherzoso

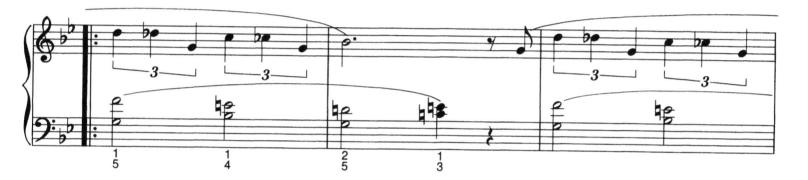

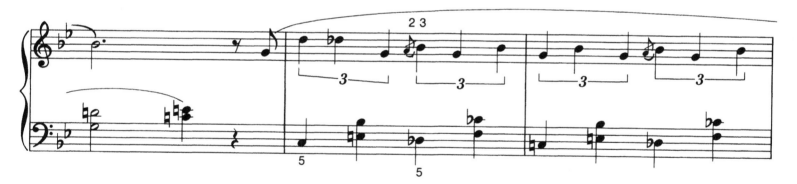

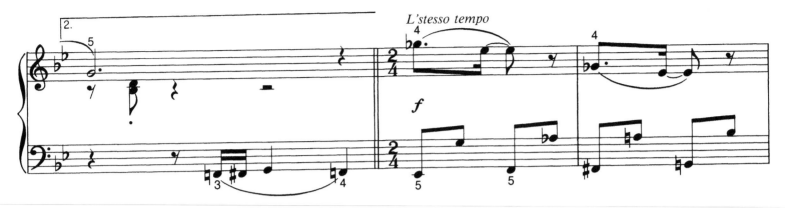

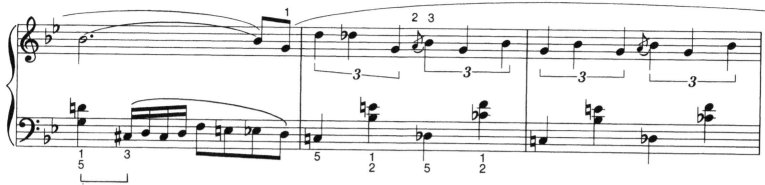

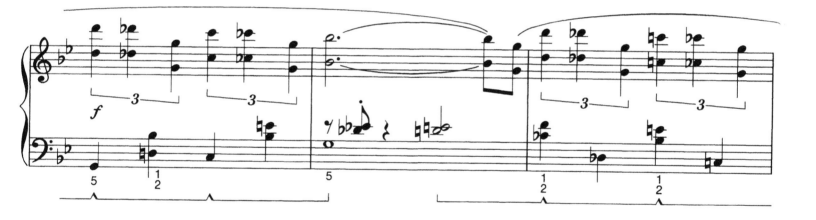

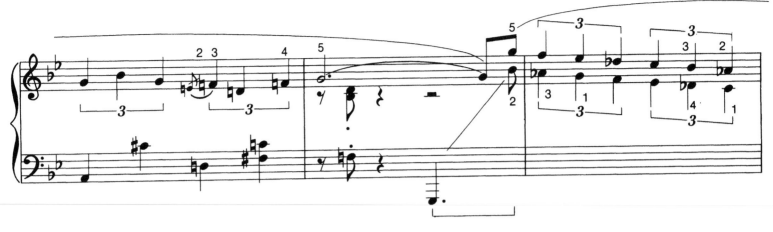

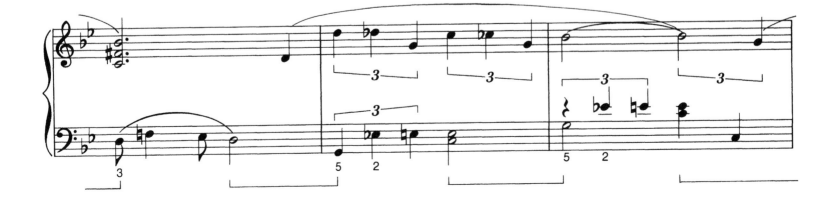

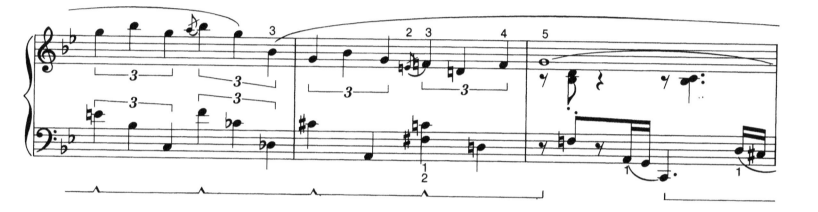

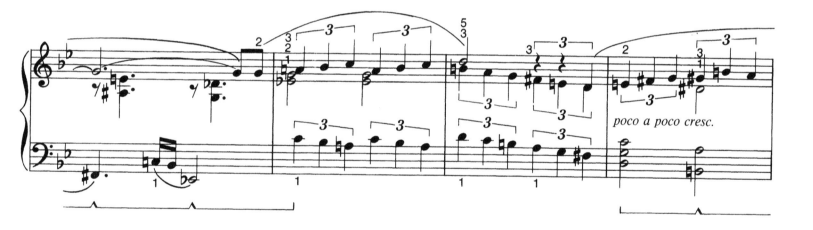

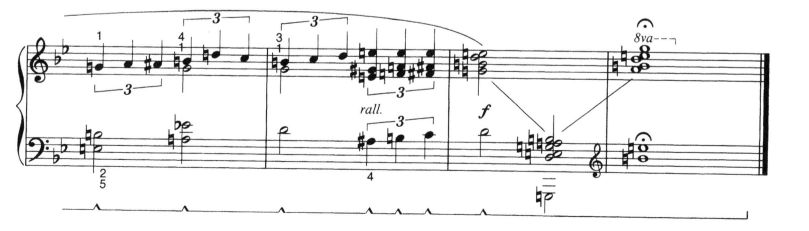

I GOT RHYTHM

Words by IRA GERSHWIN
Music by GEORGE GERSHWIN
Arranged by LEE EVANS

Exuberantly (♩ = 120)

(no pedal throughout)

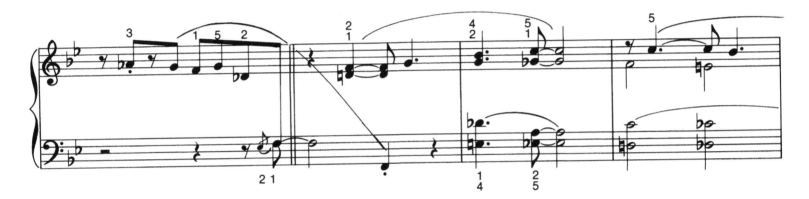

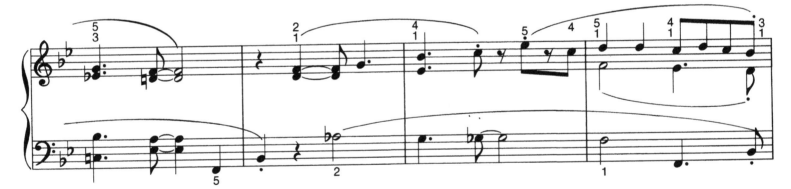

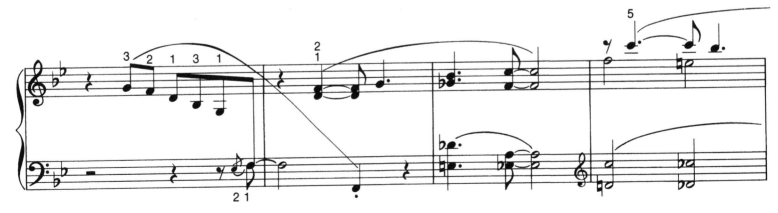

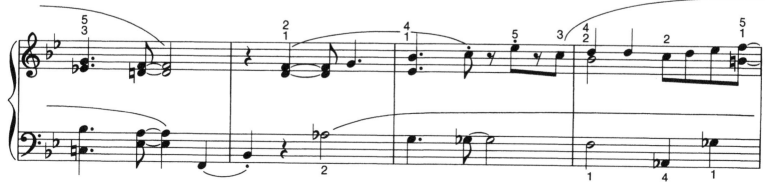

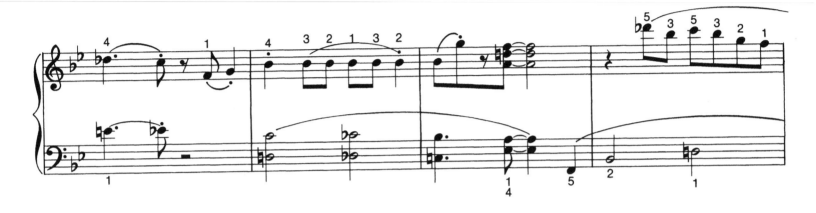

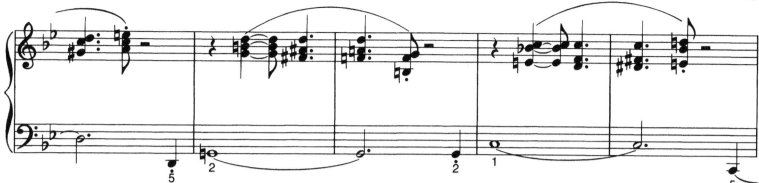

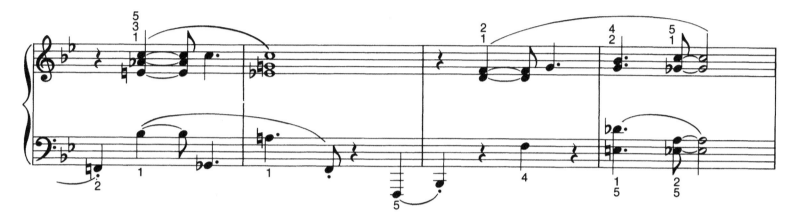

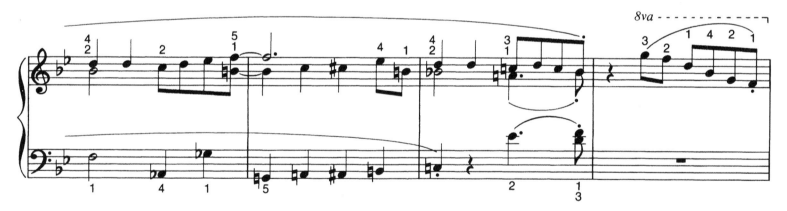

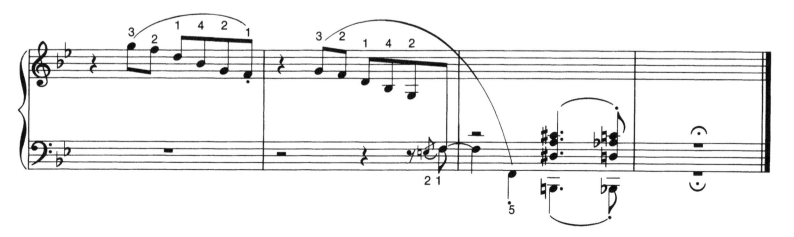

LET'S CALL THE WHOLE THING OFF

Words by IRA GERSHWIN
Music by GEORGE GERSHWIN
Arranged by LEE EVANS

Jauntily (♩ = 80)

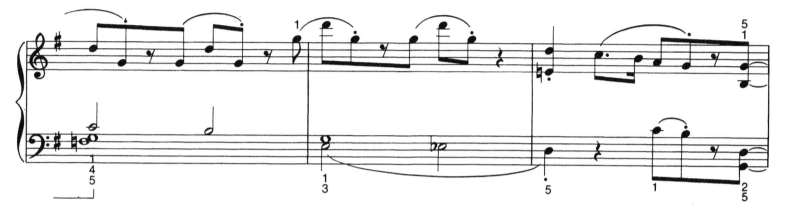

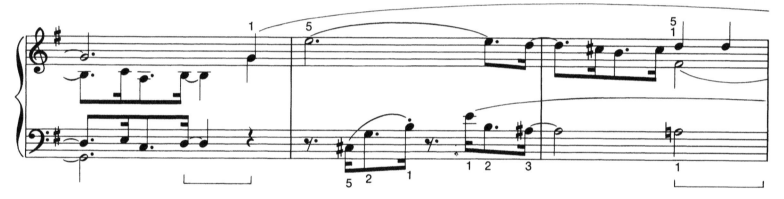

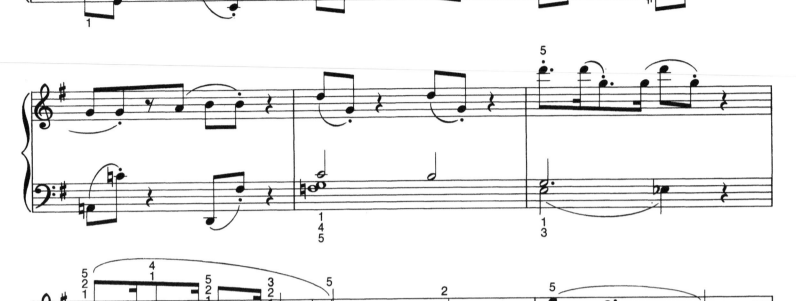

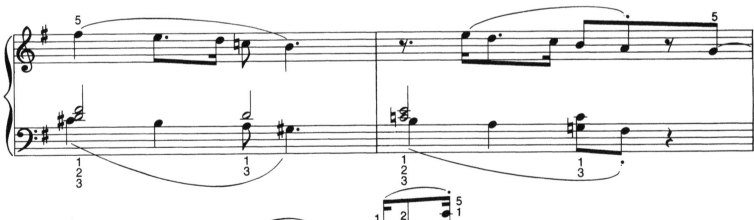

THE MAN I LOVE

Words by IRA GERSHWIN
Music by GEORGE GERSHWIN
Arranged by LEE EVANS

With simple directness (♩ = 92)

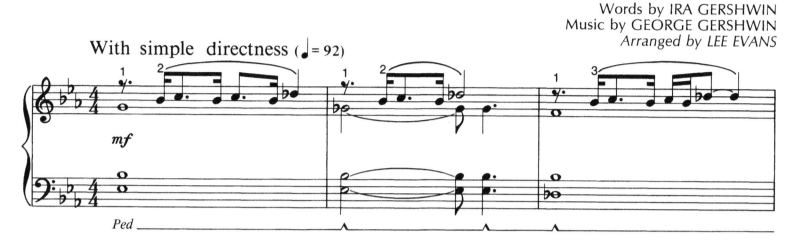

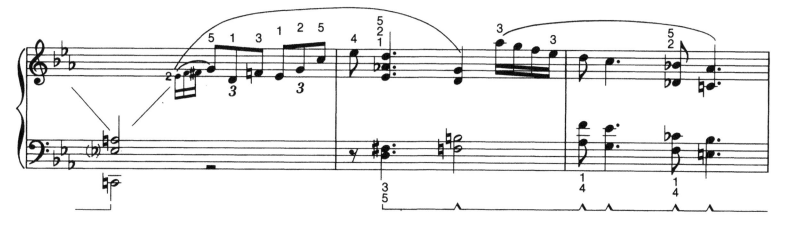

LOVE IS HERE TO STAY
(From GOLDWYN FOLLIES)

Words by IRA GERSHWIN
Music by GEORGE GERSHWIN
Arranged by LEE EVANS

With a steady beat (♩ = 120)

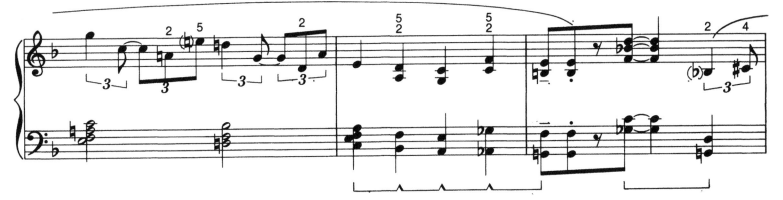

LOVE WALKED IN

Words by IRA GERSHWIN
Music by GEORGE GERSHWIN
Arranged by LEE EVANS

poco ritard

a tempo

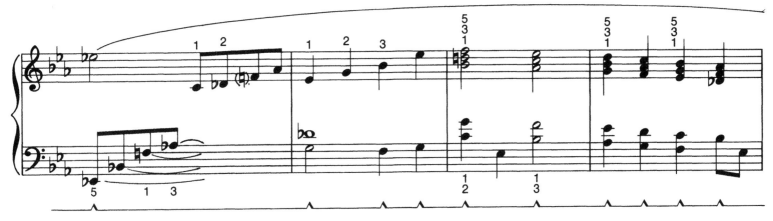

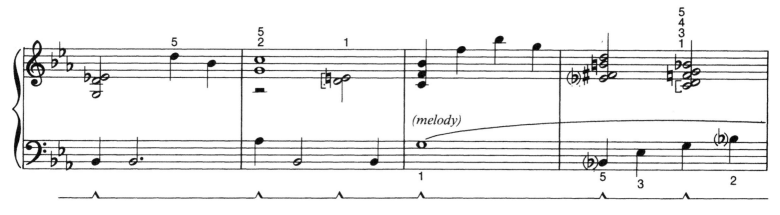

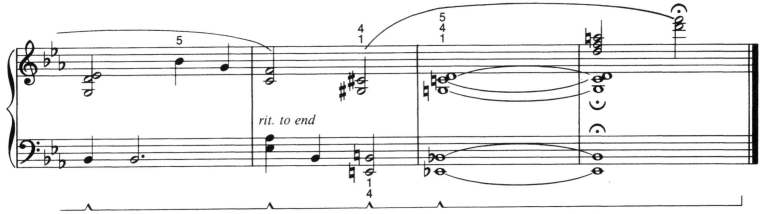

NICE WORK IF YOU CAN GET IT

Words by IRA GERSHWIN
Music by GEORGE GERSHWIN
Arranged by LEE EVANS

Medium bounce (♩ = 132)

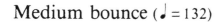

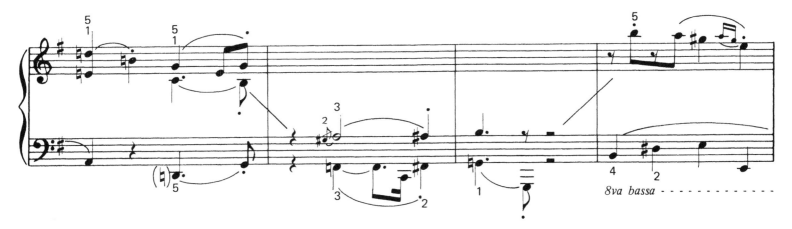

D.S. al ⊕

CODA

SOMEONE TO WATCH OVER ME

Words by IRA GERSHWIN
Music by GEORGE GERSHWIN
Arranged by LEE EVANS

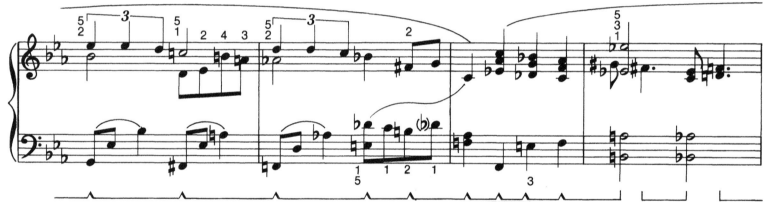

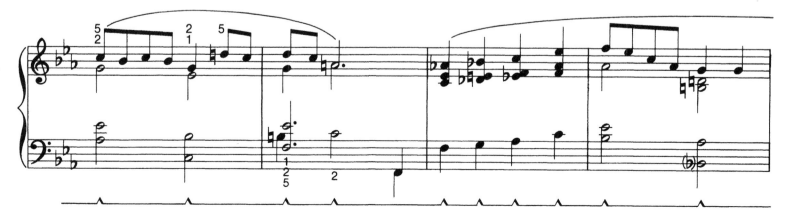

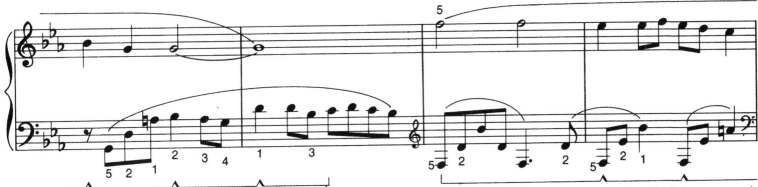

D.S. al Fine (with repeat)

rit.

a tempo

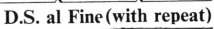

SOMEBODY LOVES ME

Words by BALLARD MACDONALD and B.G. DESYLVA
Music by GEORGE GERSHWIN
Arranged by LEE EVANS

Easy swing (♩ = 152)

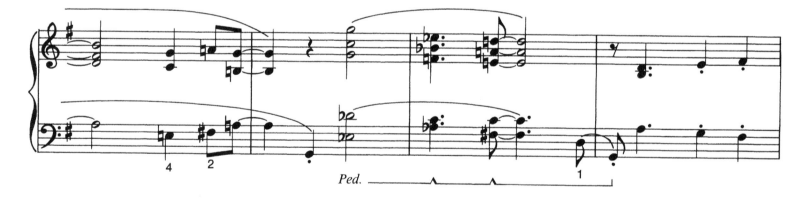

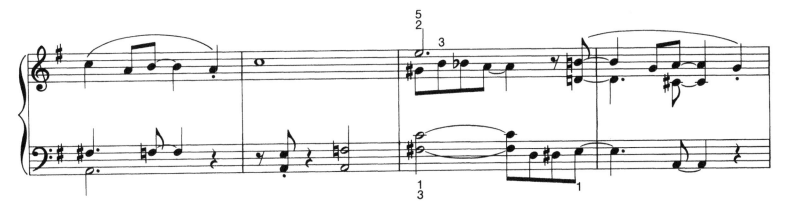

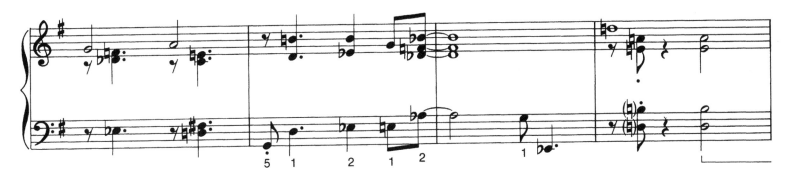

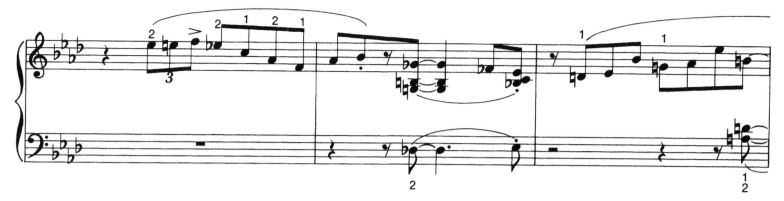

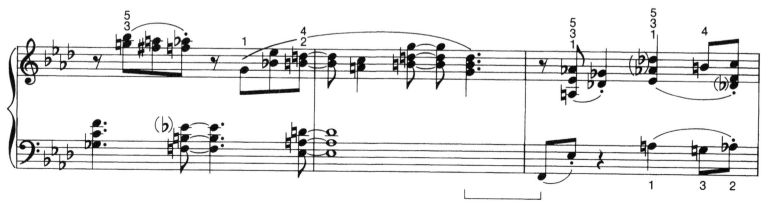

SUMMERTIME

Words by DUBOSE HEYWARD
Music by GEORGE GERSHWIN
Arranged by LEE EVANS

Moderato, rubato

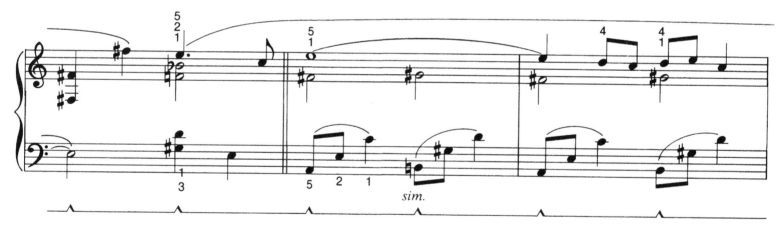

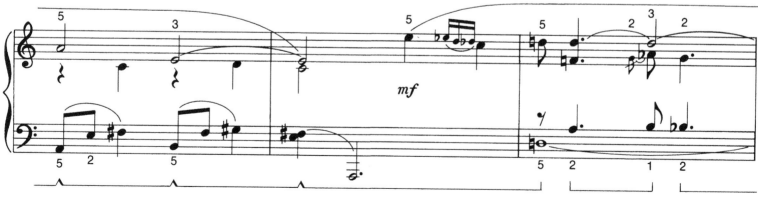

46

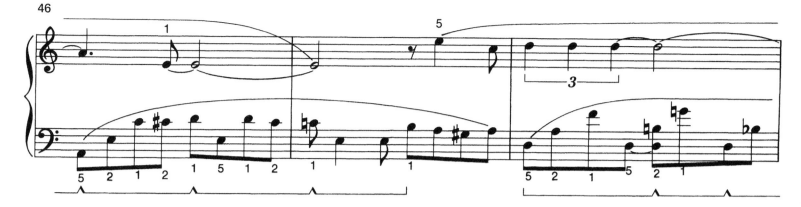

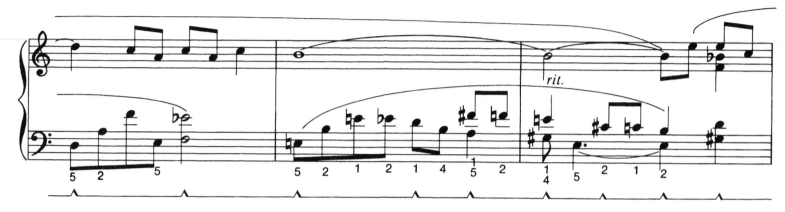

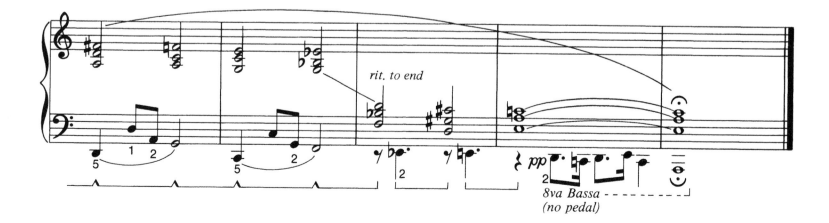

THEY ALL LAUGHED

Words by IRA GERSHWIN
Music by GEORGE GERSHWIN
Arranged by LEE EVANS

Happily (♩ = 80)

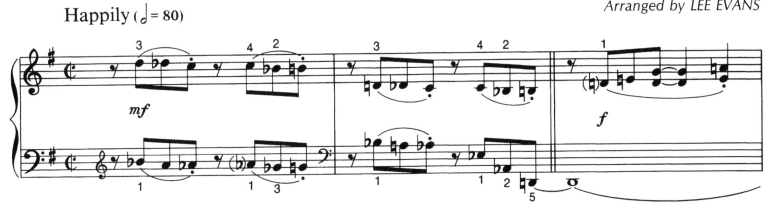

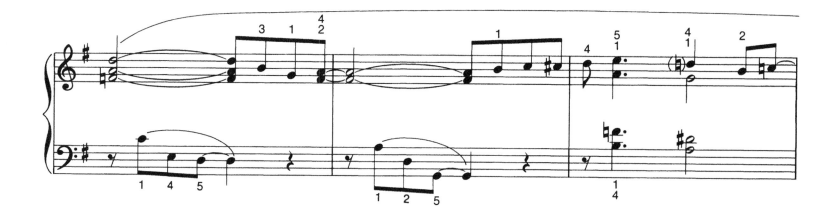

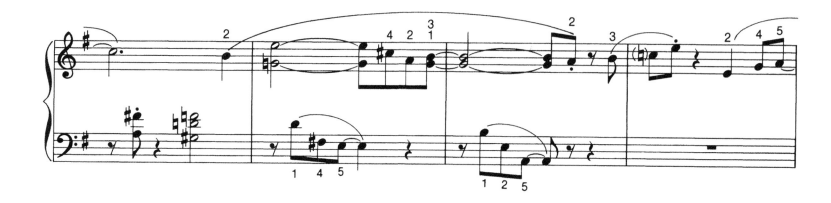

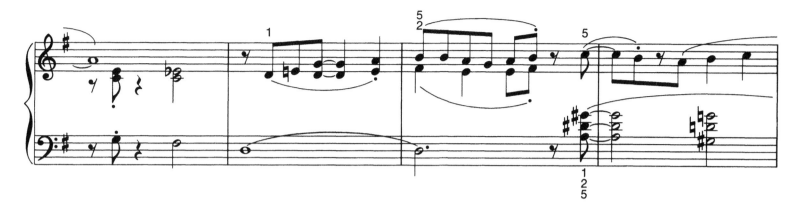

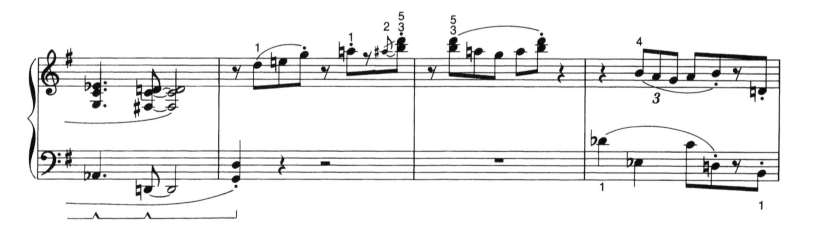

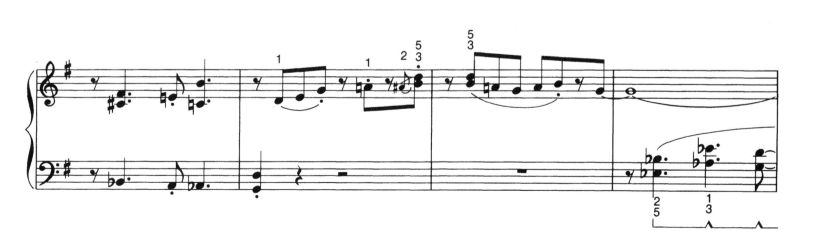

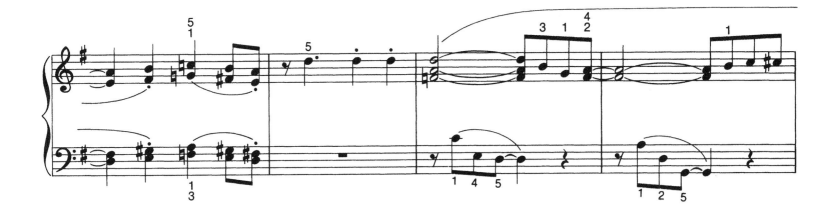

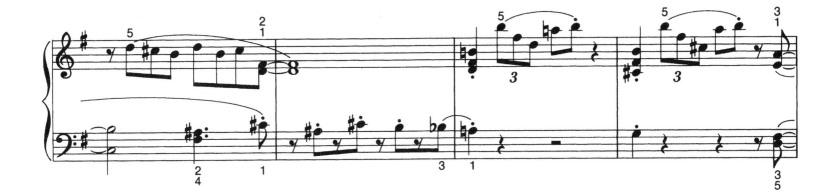

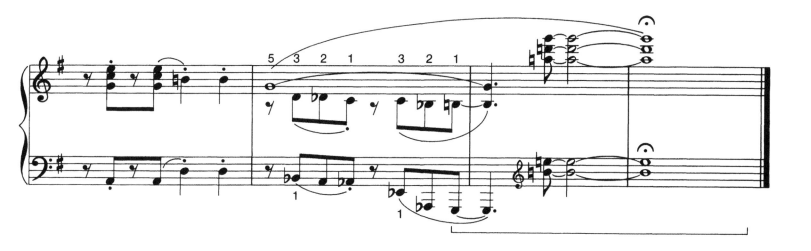

THEY CAN'T TAKE THAT AWAY FROM ME

Words by IRA GERSHWIN
Music by GEORGE GERSHWIN
Arranged by LEE EVANS

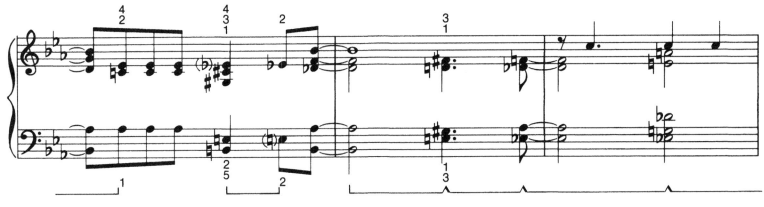

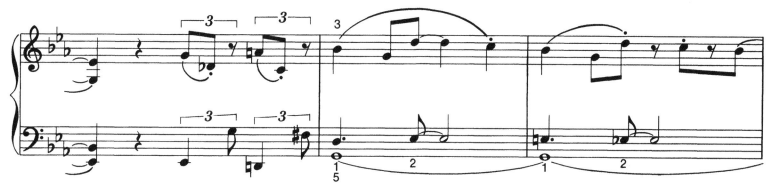

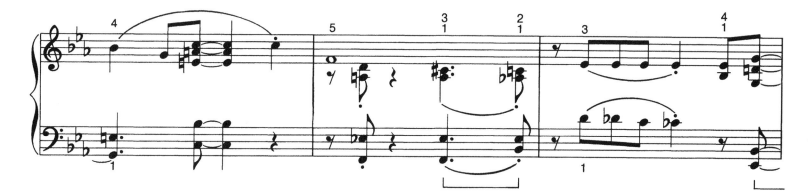

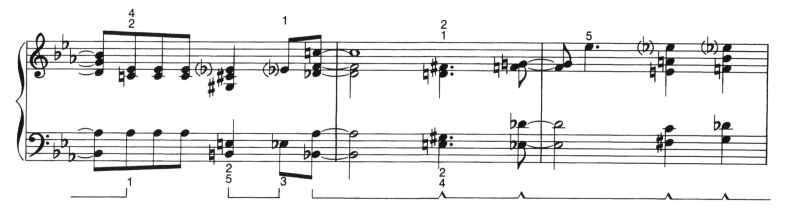

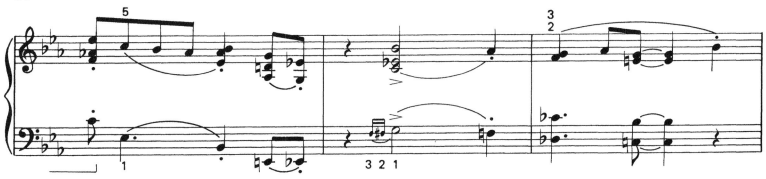

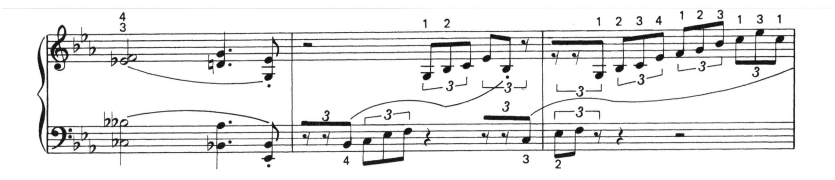

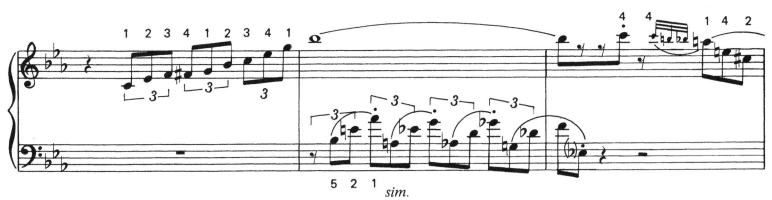

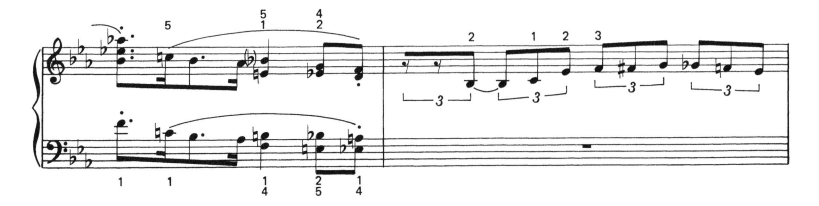

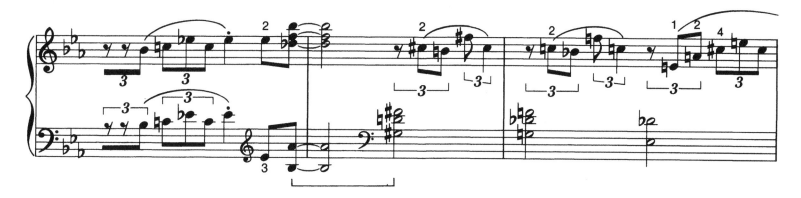

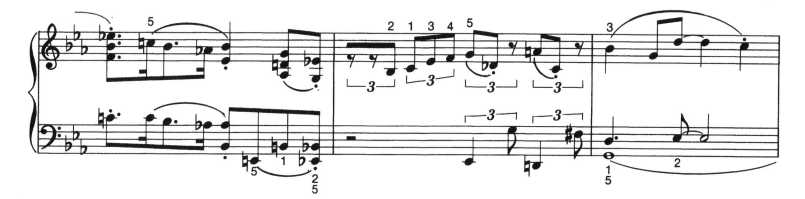

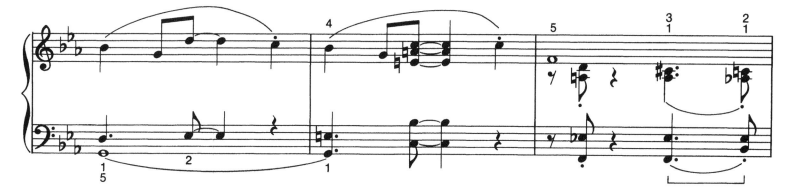

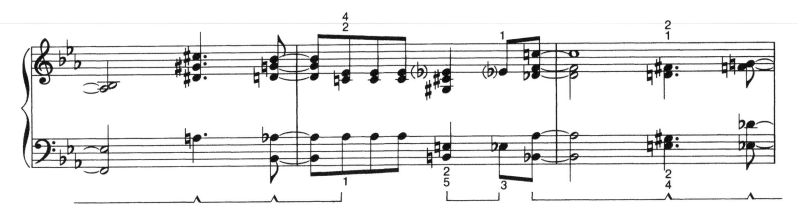

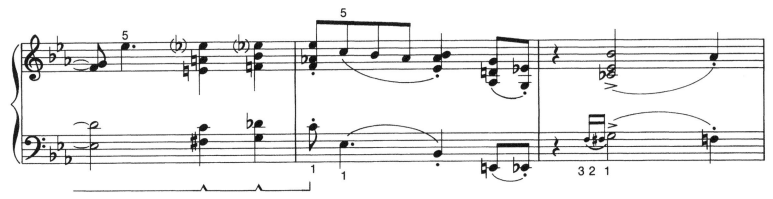

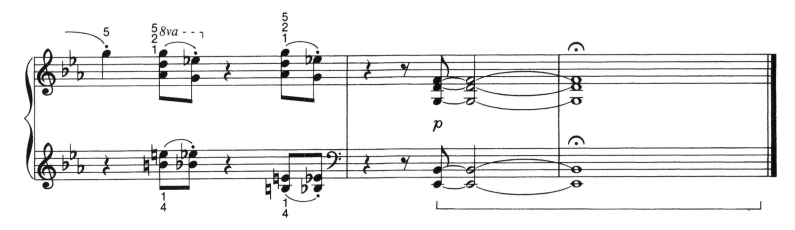